Manners
and More for Boys

Gail Reed

This Book Belongs To

_____

An Extraordinary Gentleman

of

Impeccable Character!

A Gift From

_____

For more information about the book or
to order books please visit my website

mannersbooks.com

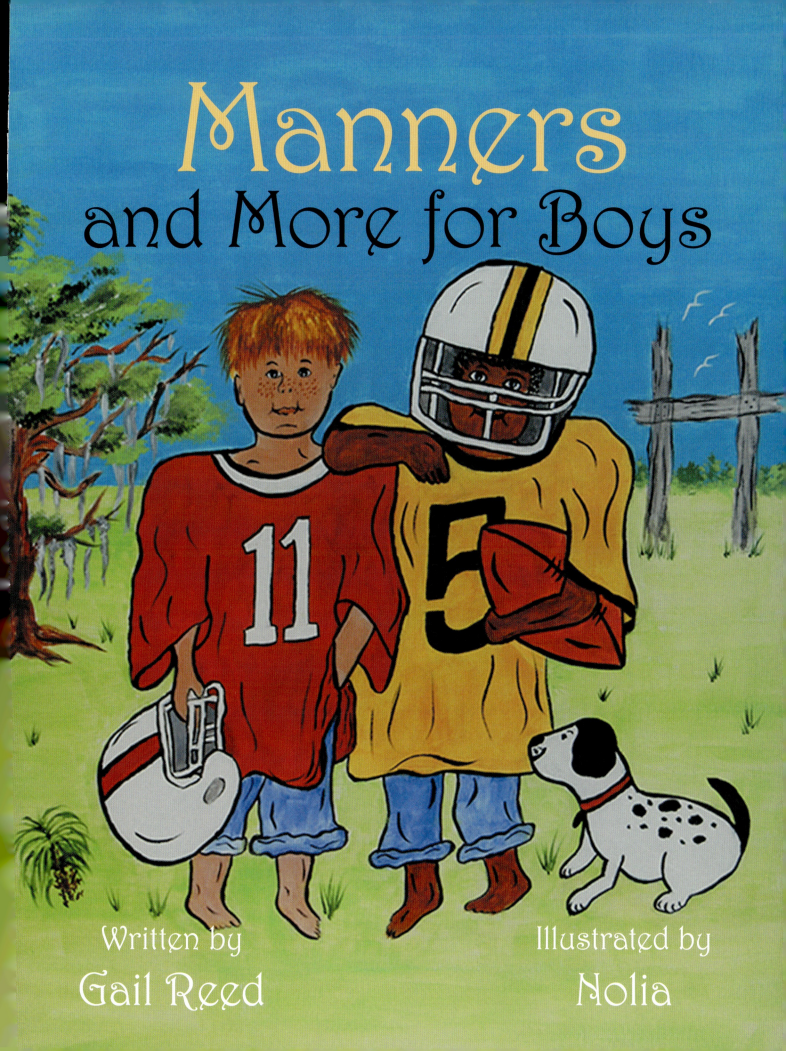

Copyright © 2015 Virginia Gail Reed.

Illustrations by Nolia.

All rights reserved. No part of this book may be used or reproduced by any means, graphic, electronic, or mechanical, including photocopying, recording, taping or by any information storage retrieval system without the written permission of the author except in the case of brief quotations embodied in critical articles and reviews.

Archway Publishing books may be ordered through booksellers or by contacting:

Archway Publishing
1663 Liberty Drive
Bloomington, IN 47403
www.archwaypublishing.com
1 (888) 242-5904

Because of the dynamic nature of the Internet, any web addresses or links contained in this book may have changed since publication and may no longer be valid. The views expressed in this work are solely those of the author and do not necessarily reflect the views of the publisher, and the publisher hereby disclaims any responsibility for them.

Any people depicted in stock imagery provided by Thinkstock are models, and such images are being used for illustrative purposes only.
Certain stock imagery © Thinkstock.

ISBN: 978-1-4808-2130-9 (sc)
ISBN: 978-1-4808-2131-6 (hc)
ISBN: 978-1-4808-2129-3 (e)

Printed in China.

Archway Publishing rev. date: 09/25/2015

Dedication

This book is dedicated to all mothers and fathers who strive to instill courteous and respectful values in their children and to the readers of this book who honor their parents by using courteous behaviors.

To my grandparents, Harold and Eula Stone, who made it possible for me to have a lifetime of special memories enjoying the Lowcountry on St. Helena Island at Lands End, South Carolina.

To the wonderful gentlemen in my life . . . my husband, Travis, my sons-in-law, Cory and Tyler, and my grandsons, Connor, Finn, and Reed.

Teaching children good manners must begin at an early age and these behaviors reinforced until they become second nature. Instilling good manners in a child is one of the most important responsibilities a parent will ever have. This book is meant to grow with your child, because teaching manners is an ongoing process. It is also meant to encourage dialogue in learning proper social behavior.

Boys can be rough and boys can be tough . . .
but boys that demonstrate courteous and polite behavior are

"Extraordinary Gentlemen!"

Using polite ways of speaking and courteous ways of acting show that you have been taught the proper rules of etiquette . . . or manners.

Rise and Shine!

Your morning routine should include brushing your teeth, washing your face, combing your hair, and showering if needed. Everyone wants to have fresh breath and smell nice and clean, so be aware of this. Dress yourself in clean clothes and do your best to look neat and presentable.

Always remember to speak to people in the morning. This includes your mother, father, sister, and brother. A simple "good morning" greeting gets your day started off on the right foot. Be sure that your friendly demeanor continues when you go to school and that you greet your teachers and friends in the same way.

Introductions and Greetings

If you are meeting a person for the first time be sure to extend your hand and give them a firm handshake. Be pleasant, use direct eye contact, and call the person by name when you tell them, "It is nice to meet you!" If you do not know their name . . . ask! Say, "Hello, my name is (your name), and what is your name?" When shaking hands, please don't let your hand feel like a limp noodle . . . grip their hand firmly and confidently. Following these simple guidelines will help you make a good first impression.

It is important for you to respond when another person enters a room or comes into your presence. You should stop what you are doing and acknowledge that person immediately.

Restroom Responsibilities

    Always knock before entering if the bathroom door is closed. Please boys . . . you must remember to aim carefully when you are using the restroom. If you have an accident and make a mess it is your responsibility to clean it up before you leave! Always lower the seat, flush the toilet, and wash and dry your hands thoroughly when finished. If you shower don't forget to hang up your towel, put your clothes in the dirty clothes hamper, and leave the area clean.

Attitude

Attitude is defined as a feeling or way of thinking that affects a person's behavior or the way you think and feel about someone or something. Disrespectful actions such as rolling your eyes, refusing to look at someone's face, and walking away while someone is talking to you are discourteous and demonstrate a poor attitude. Being cocky is not cool! Control your attitude . . . be positive and constructive in the things you say and do. Nobody likes a smart aleck or a know-it-all. Never gossip or talk about other people in a negative way. This kind of action is hurtful and unkind and you would never want to say anything about another person that you wouldn't want said about yourself.

Be a Good Sport!

Show good sportsmanship at all times. No one likes a sore loser! Tell your opponents, "good game," and don't brag if you are on the winning team. Also, never boo the opposing team . . . this shows poor sportsmanship as well as poor character!

When playing team sports show others that you are a team player by the way you conduct yourself during a game. Share the ball . . . don't be a ball hog!! Cheer for your teammates and be supportive. You play on a team . . . it's not a one-man show!

If someone steals the ball, as in basketball, or makes a good block, as in football, don't be angry just play harder. Show good sportsmanship by playing aggressively within the rules of the game.

Gentlemen . . . Please Stand Up!

When a lady enters or exits a room or if a girl comes to or leaves the dining table, a gentleman should always stand to show respect. This may seem old-fashioned, but it shows that you have courteous manners and that you are an **"Extraordinary Gentleman!"** Boys, if you are seated on a bus, train, or anywhere, and a lady or older person enters, please stand up and offer them your seat if none are available. This action is appreciated and it is what gentlemen do. Hold the door open for ladies and allow older people or children to go inside first. A good rule to remember is . . . "Ladies and babies go first!" When preceding others into a building, don't let the door slam in the face of those behind you. Instead, hold the door until it can be reached. This reflects courteous and respectful behavior!

Boys, do not wear a hat when you are indoors. Remove your hat when entering a building and put it back on when you leave.

Eye Contact and Polite Conversation

It is so important to look people directly in the eyes if you are talking to them or if they are talking to you. This visual contact with another person shows respect and that you are truly interested in what that person has to say. It also lets them know that you are sincere in what you are saying to them.

If there are several people involved in a conversation, please make sure that everyone feels included . . . no one wants to be left out of a discussion. Don't monopolize or do all of the talking . . . let others share their ideas.

Do not interrupt a person when he or she is talking. Wait for them to finish what they are saying and then speak. If someone makes a mistake, kindly point it out to him or her privately. Don't embarrass any person in front of others.

The Magic Words

Remember to say, "yes, ma'am" and "no, ma'am" or "yes, sir" and "no, sir" (or just "yes, please" and "no, thank you" if customary). These words simply show that you are being polite. Don't forget to say, "please, thank you, you're welcome, and excuse me," as these are courteous words that all refined gentlemen use.

Writing a thank-you note is another way of showing respect for someone who has done something kind for you. This lets that person know how much you appreciate their thoughtfulness. Showing gratitude by writing the individual and expressing your feelings exhibits genuine kindness and sincerity. If you receive a gift and you already have the exact same item, remember to be gracious and thank the person who gave you the present... never remark that you already have one.

The Proper Way to Treat A Girl

Boys . . . girls appreciate kindness so be sure to open the door for ladies, use proper language in their presence, offer them your chair if no other seats are available, and be helpful by offering assistance if needed. Treat a female like she is special . . . because she truly is!

Girls like to be remembered on occasions like Christmas, Valentine's Day, and birthdays. Gifts need not be expensive but should be sincere. Show that chivalrous behavior does still exist by behaving in an honorable and polite way. Boys, never forget . . . your mom is a girl!

Accepting Responsibility

Always take responsibility for the things you do. If you do something wrong admit your mistake, say you are sorry, and make every effort to prevent it from happening again. We all make mistakes, but you must acknowledge your errors and accept responsibility for your actions. If consequences are imposed, take them with a good and positive attitude and learn from the experience.

Keep your room tidy and be quick to volunteer to help around the house. You should make your bed, pick up your toys, and keep your room organized. Keep your parents informed about your schoolwork so they can assist you when you need help. It is your job to complete your homework assignments and turn them in on or before the due date. You will gain the admired distinction of being reliable by being punctual and fulfilling expectations.

Respect!

Be particularly aware of treating your elders with honor and respect. Offer them your seat and allow them to go first in line. Older people have much wisdom and you can learn many valuable lessons by taking the time to listen to what they have to say.

Remember to thank the men and women that serve in the military. Express gratitude for their service and acknowledge their contributions that keep our country free. Be aware that you may be the one wearing that uniform one day.

Be grateful for the law enforcement officers and first responders that protect you and your community. These brave individuals who strive to keep us safe deserve our gratitude and respect.

Self-Control and Communication Skills

    Don't lose your temper easily or use language that is inappropriate as this shows poor self-control. Instead, learn to manage your emotions in a positive way. The use of offensive language is never appropriate as it only reveals poor character and a limited vocabulary. DO NOT tattle on others (unless they are in danger), spread rumors that hurt people, or make fun of people who are different. Be aware of what your body language is saying . . . clinching your fist, stamping your feet, having a scowl on your face, or pouting shows poor self-control. When shopping with your parents make sure to stay close, don't plead for toys, or run and play in the store. Show that you are well behaved by using self-control.

    Effective face-to-face communication skills are essential to success in life. The ability to convey your thoughts and feelings is important. Be aware that words such as "like" and "you know" are often overused. Be certain that the words you use are chosen carefully and intelligently . . . think before you speak. You should NOT play video games, text, or talk on the phone in inappropriate places.

Table Manners

Before a meal, always remove your hat and it would be considerate to offer to help set the table. Before you sit always wait for ladies and elders to be seated. Place your napkin in your lap, and you should not start eating until everyone else has been served. Use nice table manners . . . DO NOT place your elbows on the table, chew with your mouth open, speak with food in your mouth, or discuss inappropriate topics. Pass food as requested from left to right and never say that you don't like a particular dish. Just say, "I don't care for any thank you." When finished, place your napkin beside your plate, your utensils across your plate, and always tell your host or hostess that you enjoyed the meal. It would be thoughtful to offer to help clear the table.

When dining out, do not disturb other people who are there to enjoy their meal. Remain in your seat, speak in a quiet tone, stay off of your cell phone or electronic devices, and show courtesy toward the person serving you. Polite manners are expected from a *gentleman* . . . and that is exactly what you are!

Bullying

Stand up for a person that is being put down or bullied. DO NOT allow bullying to take place at any time when you are with your friends or acquaintances. Support your friends and inspire them. However, please be aware that you must always be certain that your friend's words and actions are worthy of your encouragement and support. When in doubt, always choose to be kind. This includes your communications on social media. Cyber-bullying that involves inappropriate texts or email is NEVER acceptable. If you receive a threatening electronic communication from anyone, seek assistance from an adult as soon as possible. Never be afraid to stand up for what is right!

Decisions . . . Decisions!

You make many choices every day. You decide what food you will eat, whether or not you will do your homework, or how you spend your free time. The choices you make define your character and become your life. You know right from wrong and you know good from bad. Don't be afraid to ask an adult for guidance.

Be a good role model. Others are watching and learning from your actions. Choose your friends with care. Friends should bring out the best in you. Make your own choices . . . don't follow others blindly.

Good Character is Important!

Character is defined as the way someone thinks, feels, and behaves. Simply put, it is the way you act when no one is looking. Having good character indicates moral strength and is a positive personality trait. The friends you make, how successful you are in the career path you select, and even the attraction of your ideal spouse later in life will be determined by your character and good manners. The polite way that you treat others and the courteous actions you choose will put you on an appropriate and positive path in life. Your character is reflected in the way you treat your fellow man. Always treat others with kindness, respect, and civility. Our world would be so much better if everyone practiced this! Strive to be the best that you can be and take great pride in all that you do.

Honor your Mother and Father, or that special person who takes care of you, by being kind and considerate to others. You can be strong and athletic and still have a tender and compassionate heart by the way you act and how you treat other people.

Yes, boys can be rough and boys can be tough . . .

but using courteous and polite skills, which are known as proper etiquette or good manners, will easily identify you as an . . .

"Extraordinary Gentleman!"

Making others feel comfortable is the essence of etiquette.

In The List Below, Which Manners Do You Know And Use Every Day?

I speak to people in the morning.
I brush my teeth and keep my body clean.
I look people in the eyes when I talk to them.
I give a firm handshake when I meet someone.

I knock before entering a room when the door is closed.
I leave the bathroom neat and clean.
I do not roll my eyes when I disagree with a person.
I do not act like a smart aleck or a know-it-all.

I keep my mouth closed if I don't have a kind word to say.
I do not walk away from a person that is talking to me.
I am a good sport and congratulate the team that wins.
I do not boo the opposing team or have unkind things to say.

I do not brag if my team wins.
I do not hog the ball and try to be a team player at all times.
I stand up if a lady enters or leaves the room.
I remember the rule, "Ladies and babies go first!"

I do not wear a hat indoors.
I do not tattle on my friends unless there is danger involved.
I offer ladies and my elders a chair if they do not have one.
I try to include all people that are involved in a discussion.

I say, "Yes, ma'am, no, ma'am, yes, sir, and no, sir, or yes/no."
I write thank-you notes when I receive a gift.
I say, "Please, thank you, you're welcome, and excuse me."
I use proper language in the presence of ladies and friends.

I take responsibility for the things I say and do.
I make up my bed and keep my room tidy.
I help out with chores around the house.
I turn in assignments on time and take pride in a job well-done.

I inform my parents of deadlines that are coming up.
I show respect to adults, seniors, and those in uniform.
I control my body language and use self-control at all times.
I never make fun of people who are different.

I don't plead for toys or run and play in stores.
I use my electronic devices and cell phone in appropriate places.
I strive to be on time for all commitments.
I don't use electronic devices during a meal.

I do not overuse words such as "like" or "you know."
I seat ladies and wait until everyone is served before eating.
I do not allow bullying to take place in my presence.
I tell my parents if I receive improper texts, email, or tweets.

I try to make good choices knowing that it will affect my future.
I treat other people with courtesy and respect.
I stop what I am doing and acknowledge a person that enters.
I honor my Mother and Father by being kind and considerate.

I can be physically strong and athletic and still have a compassionate heart.

I can and will be an *"Extraordinary Gentleman!"*

Second in a series of five books on manners
for children, teens, and adults.

I Can't Find My Manners

Manners and More for Boys

Manners and More for Girls

Manners and More for Little Ones

Manners at the Theater for Young People

Gail Reed
Author

About the Author

Gail Reed, a retired educator of forty-two years, lives in Evans, Georgia, with her husband, Travis. She grew up spending summers in the Lowcountry with her grandparents, Meme and Papa, at their beach house at Lands End, South Carolina. Many happy hours were spent fishing, crabbing, and skiing in the waters of St. Helena Sound. She still enjoys time at this beach house that is shared with her family. Due to her love of the area, the artwork of this second book has a Lowcountry theme.